BY ADRIENNE RICH

Time's Power: Poems 1985–1988

Blood, Bread, and Poetry: Selected Prose 1979–1986

Your Native Land, Your Life

The Fact of a Doorframe:
Poems Selected and New 1950–1984

Sources

A Wild Patience Has Taken Me This Far

On Lies, Secrets, and Silence: Selected Prose, 1966–1978

The Dream of a Common Language

Twenty-one Love Poems

Of Woman Born: Motherhood
As Experience and Institution

Poems: Selected and New, 1950–1974

Diving into the Wreck

The Will to Change

Leaflets

Necessities of Life

Snapshots of a Daughter-in-Law

The Diamond Cutters

A Change of World

AN ATLAS OF
THE DIFFICULT
WORLD

W·W·NORTON & COMPANY
NEW YORK · LONDON

AN ATLAS OF THE DIFFICULT WORLD

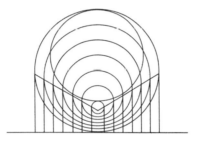

POEMS 1988–1991

ADRIENNE RICH

Grateful acknowledgment is made for permission to quote from the following: George Jackson, *Soledad Brother: The Prison Letters of George Jackson* (New York: Bantam Books, 1970).

These poems were originally published in the following journals and magazines:

American Poetry Review—"An Atlas of the Difficult World," I, II, IV, V, VI.
Bastard Review—"That Mouth" and "Olivia."
Beloit Poetry Journal (Fortieth Anniversary Issue)—"Marghanita."
Bridges: A Journal for Jewish Feminists and Our Friends—"An Atlas of the Difficult World," XI, XIII; "Eastern War Time."
Field: Contemporary Poetry and Poetics—"Through Corralitos Under Rolls of Cloud."
Frontiers: A Journal of Women's Studies—"An Atlas of the Difficult World," X, XII; "1948: Jews."
Ms.—"She."
Poetry—"Final Notations," "For a Friend in Travail," "Two Arts."

Printed in the United States of America.

The text of this book is composed in Garamond No. 3
with the display set in Bauer Text Initials
Composition by PennSet, Inc.
Manufacturing by Colvier Companies Inc.
Book design by Antonina Krass

Library of Congress Cataloging in Publication Data
Rich, Adrienne Cecile.
An atlas of the difficult world: poems, 1988–1991 / Adrienne
Rich.
p. cm.
I. Title.
PS3535.I233A84   1991
811'.54—dc20   91–12900

ISBN 0-393-03069-5
ISBN 0-393-30831-6 (pbk)

W. W. Norton & Company, Inc., 500 Fifth Avenue, New York, NY 10110
W. W. Norton & Company, Ltd., 10 Coptic Street, London WC1A 1PU

2 3 4 5 6 7 8 9 0

—for John Benedict, in memory—

CONTENTS

I

AN ATLAS OF THE DIFFICULT WORLD

I.	A dark woman, head bent, listening for something	3
II.	Here is a map of our country:	6
III.	Two five-pointed star-shaped glass candleholders . . .	7
IV.	Late summers, early autumns, you can see something that binds	11
V.	Catch if you can your country's moment, begin	12
VI.	A potato explodes in the oven. Poetry and famine:	15
VII.	(*The dream-site*) Some rooftop, water-tank looming, street-racket strangely quelled	16
VIII.	He thought there would be a limit and that it would stop him. He depended on that:	17
IX.	On this earth, in this life, as I read your story, you're lonely.	19
X.	*Soledad.* = f. *Solitude, loneliness, homesickness; lonely retreat.*	20
XI.	One night on Monterey Bay the death-freeze of the century:	22
XII.	What homage will be paid to a beauty built to last	24
XIII.	(*Dedications*) I know you are reading this poem	25

II

She	29
That Mouth	30
Marghanita	31
Olivia	33

Eastern War Time   35
   1. Memory lifts her smoky mirror: 1943,   35
   2. Girl between home and school   what is that girl   36
   3. How telegrams used to come: ring   37
   4. What the grown-ups can't speak of   would you push 38
   5. A young girl knows she is young and meant to live   39
   6. A girl wanders with a boy into the woods   40
   7. A woman of sixty   driving   41
   8. A woman wired in memories   42
   9. Streets closed, emptied by force   Guns at corners 43
  10. Memory says: Want to do right? Don't count on me.   44
Tattered Kaddish   45
Through Corralitos Under Rolls of Cloud   46
   I. Through Corralitos under rolls of cloud   46
  II. Showering after 'flu;   stripping the bed;   47
 III. If you know who died in that bed, do you know   48
 IV. That light of outrage is the light of history   49
  V. She who died on that bed sees it her way: 50
For a Friend in Travail   51
1948:   Jews   52
Two Arts   53
   1. I've redone you by daylight.   53
   2. Raise it up there and it will   54
Darklight   55
   I. Early day.   Grey the air.   55
  II. When heat leaves the walls at last   56
Final Notations   57

Notes   59

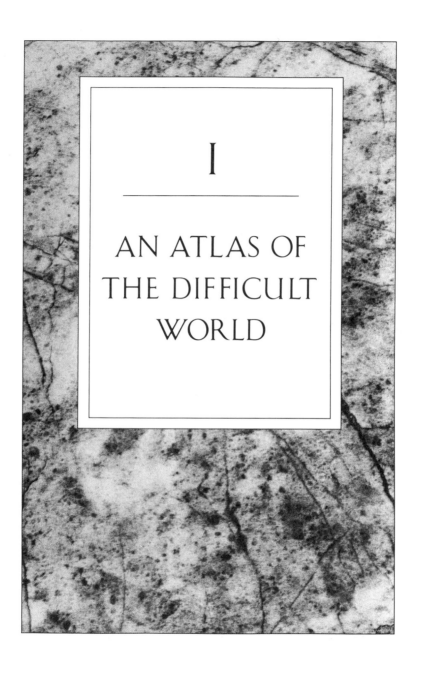

I

AN ATLAS OF THE DIFFICULT WORLD

I

A dark woman, head bent, listening for something
—a woman's voice, a man's voice or
voice of the freeway, night after night, metal streaming downcoast
past eucalyptus, cypress, agribusiness empires
THE SALAD BOWL OF THE WORLD, gurr of small planes
dusting the strawberries, each berry picked by a hand
in close communion, strawberry blood on the wrist,
Malathion in the throat, communion,
the hospital at the edge of the fields,
prematures slipping from unsafe wombs,
the labor and delivery nurse on her break watching
planes dusting rows of pickers.
Elsewhere declarations are made: at the sink
rinsing strawberries flocked and gleaming, fresh from market
one says: "On the pond this evening is a light
finer than my mother's handkerchief
received from her mother, hemmed and initialled
by the nuns in Belgium."
One says: "I can lie for hours
reading and listening to music. But sleep comes hard.
I'd rather lie awake and read."   One writes:
"Mosquitoes pour through the cracks
in this cabin's walls, the road
in winter is often impassable,
I live here so I don't have to go out and act,
I'm trying to hold onto my life, it feels like nothing."
One says: "I never knew from one day to the next
where it was coming from: I had to make my life happen
from day to day.   Every day an emergency.
Now I have a house, a job from year to year.
What does that make me?"

3

In the writing workshop a young man's tears
wet the frugal beard he's grown to go with his poems
hoping they have redemption stored
in their lines, maybe will get him home free.   In the classroom
eight-year-old faces are grey.   The teacher knows which children
have not broken fast that day,
remembers the Black Panthers spooning cereal.

———————O———————

I don't want to hear how he beat her after the earthquake,
tore up her writing, threw the kerosene
lantern into her face waiting
like an unbearable mirror of his own.   I don't
want to hear how she finally ran from the trailer
how he tore the keys from her hands, jumped into the truck
and backed it into her.   I don't want to think
how her guesses betrayed her—that he meant well, that she
was really the stronger and ought not to leave him
to his own apparent devastation.   I don't want to know
wreckage, dreck and waste, but these are the materials
and so are the slow lift of the moon's belly
over wreckage, dreck, and waste, wild treefrogs calling in
another season, light and music still pouring over
our fissured, cracked terrain.

———————O———————

Within two miles of the Pacific rounding
this long bay, sheening the light for miles
inland, floating its fog through redwood rifts and over
strawberry and artichoke fields, its bottomless mind
returning always to the same rocks, the same cliffs, with
ever-changing words, always the same language
—this is where I live now.   If you had known me
once, you'd still know me now though in a different
light and life.   This is no place you ever knew me.

4

But it would not surprise you
to find me here, walking in fog, the sweep of the great ocean
eluding me, even the curve of the bay, because as always
I fix on the land.   I am stuck to earth.   What I love here
is old ranches, leaning seaward, lowroofed spreads between rocks
small canyons running through pitched hillsides
liveoaks twisted on steepness, the eucalyptus avenue leading
to the wrecked homestead, the fogwreathed heavy-chested cattle
on their blond hills.   I drive inland over roads
closed in wet weather, past shacks hunched in the canyons
roads that crawl down into darkness and wind into light
where trucks have crashed and riders of horses tangled
to death with lowstruck boughs.   These are not the roads
you knew me by.   But the woman driving, walking, watching
for life and death, is the same.

5

II

Here is a map of our country:
here is the Sea of Indifference, glazed with salt
This is the haunted river flowing from brow to groin
we dare not taste its water
This is the desert where missiles are planted like corms
This is the breadbasket of foreclosed farms
This is the birthplace of the rockabilly boy
This is the cemetery of the poor
who died for democracy   This is a battlefield
from a nineteenth-century war   the shrine is famous
This is the sea-town of myth and story   when the fishing fleets
went bankrupt   here is where the jobs were   on the pier
processing frozen fishsticks   hourly wages and no shares
These are other battlefields   Centralia   Detroit
here are the forests primeval   the copper   the silver lodes
These are the suburbs of acquiescence   silence rising fumelike
                    from the streets
This is the capital of money and dolor whose spires
flare up through air inversions whose bridges are crumbling
whose children are drifting blind alleys pent
between coiled rolls of razor wire
I promised to show you a map you say but this is a mural
then yes let it be   these are small distinctions
where do we see it from is the question

III

Two five-pointed star-shaped glass candleholders, bought at the
        Ben Franklin, Barton, twenty-three years ago, one
        chipped
—now they hold half-burnt darkred candles, and in between
a spider is working, the third point of her filamental passage
a wicker basket-handle.   All afternoon I've sat
at this table in Vermont, reading, writing, cutting an apple in
        slivers
and eating them, but mostly gazing down through the windows
at the long scribble of lake due south
where the wind and weather come from.   There are bottles set in
        the windows
that children dug up in summer woods or bought for nickels and
        dimes
in dark shops that are no more, gold-brown, foam-green or cobalt
        glass, blue that gave way to the cobalt
        bomb.   The woods
are still on the hill behind the difficult unknowable
incommensurable barn.   The wind's been working itself up
in low gusts gnashing the leaves left chattering on branches
or drifting over still-green grass;   but it's been a warm wind.
An autumn without a killing frost so far, still warm
feels like a time of self-deception, a memory of pushing
limits in youth, that intricate losing game of innocence long
        overdue.
Frost is expected tonight, gardens are gleaned, potplants taken
        in, there is talk of withering, of wintering-over.

——————————O——————————

North of Willoughby the back road to Barton
turns a right-hand corner on a high plateau
bitten by wind now and rimed grey-white

7

—farms of rust and stripping paint, the shortest growing season
south of Quebec, a place of sheer unpretentious hardship, dark
                    pines stretching away
toward Canada.   There was a one-room schoolhouse
by a brook where we used to picnic, summers, a little world
of clear bubbling water, cowturds, moss, wild mint, wild mush-
                    rooms under the pines.
One hot afternoon I sat there reading Gaskell's *Life of Charlotte
                    Brontë*—the remote
upland village where snow lay long and late, the deep-rutted
                    roads, the dun and grey moorland
—trying to enfigure such a life, how genius
unfurled in the shortlit days, the meagre means of that house. I
                    never thought
of lives at that moment around me, what girl dreamed
and was extinguished in the remote back-country I had come to
                    love,
reader reading under a summer tree in the landscape
of the rural working poor.

Now the panes are black and from the south the wind still stag-
                    gers, creaking the house:
brown milkweeds toss in darkness below but I cannot see them
the room has lost the window and turned into itself: two corner
                    shelves of things
both useful and unused, things arrived here by chance or choice,
                    two teapots, one broken-spouted, red and blue
came to me with some books from my mother's mother, my
                    grandmother Mary
who travelled little, loved the far and strange, bits of India, Asia
and this teapot of hers was Chinese or she thought it was
—the other given by a German Jew, a refugee who killed herself:
Midlands flowered ware, and this too cannot be used because
                    coated inside—why?—with flaking paint:

"You will always use it for flowers," she instructed when she
          gave it.
In a small frame, under glass, my father's bookplate, engraved in
          his ardent youth, the cleft tree-trunk and the win-
          tering ants:
Without labor, no sweetness—motto I breathed in from him and
          learned in grief and rebellion to take and use
—and later learned that not all labor ends in sweetness.
A little handwrought iron candlestick, given by another German
          woman
who hidden survived the Russian soldiers beating the walls in
          1945,
emigrated, married a poet.   I sat many times at their table.
          They are now long apart.
Some odd glasses for wine or brandy, from an ignorant, passion-
          ate time—we were in our twenties—
with the father of the children who dug for old medicine bottles
          in the woods
—afternoons listening to records, reading Karl Shapiro's *Poems of
          a Jew* and Auden's "In Sickness and in Health"
          aloud, using the poems to talk to each other
—now it's twenty years since last I heard that intake
of living breath, as if language were too much to bear,
that voice overcast like klezmer with echoes, uneven, edged,
          torn, Brooklyn street crowding Harvard Yard
—I'd have known any syllable anywhere.

Stepped out onto the night-porch.   That wind has changed,
          though still from the south
it's blowing up hard now, no longer close to earth but driving
          high
into the crowns of the maples, into my face
almost slamming the stormdoor into me.   But it's warm, warm,
pneumonia wind, death of innocence wind, unwinding wind,
time-hurtling wind.   And it has a voice in the house.   I hear

9

conversations that can't be happening, overhead in the bedrooms
and I'm not talking of ghosts.   The ghosts are here of course but
        they speak plainly
—haven't I offered food and wine, listened well for them all
        these years,
not only those known in life but those before our time
of self-deception, our intricate losing game of innocence long
        overdue?

---------------O---------------

The spider's decision is made, her path cast, candle-wick to
        wicker handle to candle,
in the air, under the lamp, she comes swimming toward me
(have I been sitting here so long?)   she will use everything,
                nothing comes without labor, she is working so
                hard and I know
nothing all winter can enter this house or this web, not all labor
        ends in sweetness.
But how do I know what she needs?   Maybe simply
to spin herself a house within a house, on her own terms
in cold, in silence.

IV

Late summers, early autumns, you can see something that binds
the map of this country together: the girasol, orange gold-
                petalled
with her black eye, laces the roadsides from Vermont to
                California
runs the edges of orchards, chain-link fences
milo fields and malls, schoolyards and reservations
truckstops and quarries, grazing ranges, graveyards
of veterans, graveyards of cars hulked and sunk, her tubers the
                jerusalem artichoke
that has fed the Indians, fed the hobos, could feed us all.
Is there anything in the soil, cross-country, that makes for
a plant so generous?   *Spendthrift* we say, as if
accounting nature's waste.   Ours darkens
the states to their strict borders, flushes
down borderless streams, leaches from lakes to the curdled foam
down by the riverside.

Waste.   Waste.   The watcher's eye put out, hands of the
                builder severed, brain of the maker starved
those who could bind, join, reweave, cohere, replenish
now at risk in this segregate republic
locked away out of sight and hearing, out of mind, shunted aside
those needed to teach, advise, persuade, weigh arguments
those urgently needed for the work of perception
work of the poet, the astronomer, the historian, the architect of
                new streets
work of the speaker who also listens
meticulous delicate work of reaching the heart of the desperate
                woman, the desperate man
—never-to-be-finished, still unbegun work of repair—it cannot
                be done without them
and where are they now?

11

V

Catch if you can your country's moment, begin
where any calendar's ripped-off: Appomattox
Wounded Knee, Los Alamos, Selma, the last airlift from Saigon
the ex-Army nurse hitch-hiking from the debriefing center; medal
             of spit on the veteran's shoulder
—catch if you can this unbound land these states without a cause
earth of despoiled graves and grazing these embittered brooks
these pilgrim ants pouring out from the bronze eyes, ears,
             nostrils,
the mouth of Liberty
             over the chained bay waters
                             San Quentin:
once we lost our way and drove in under the searchlights to the
             gates
end of visiting hours, women piling into cars
the bleak glare aching over all
                    Where are we moored?   What
                    are the bindings?   What be-
                    hooves us?

Driving the San Francisco–Oakland Bay Bridge
no monument's in sight but fog
prowling Angel Island muffling Alcatraz
poems in Cantonese inscribed on fog
no icon lifts a lamp here
history's breath blotting the air
over Gold Mountain   a transfer
of patterns like the transfer of African appliqué
to rural Alabama   voices alive in legends, curses
tongue-lashings
             poems on a weary wall

And when light swivels off Angel Island and Alcatraz
when the bays leap into life
                        views of the Palace of Fine Arts,
                        TransAmerica
when sunset bathes the three bridges
                                    still
old ghosts crouch hoarsely whispering
under Gold Mountain

North and east of the romantic headlands there are roads into tule
            fog
places where life is cheap poor quick unmonumented
Rukeyser would have guessed it coming West for the opening
of the great red bridge   *There are roads to take* she wrote
when you think of your country   driving south
to West Virginia Gauley Bridge silicon mines the flakes of it
            heaped like snow, death-angel white
—poet journalist pioneer mother
uncovering her country: *there are roads to take*

I don't want to know how he tracked them
along the Appalachian Trail, hid close
by their tent, pitched as they thought in seclusion
killing one woman, the other
dragging herself into town   his defense they had teased his
                              loathing
of what they were   I don't want to know
but this is not a bad dream of mine   these are the materials
and so are the smell of wild mint and coursing water remembered
and the sweet salt darkred tissue I lay my face
upon, my tongue within.
                         A crosshair against the pupil of an eye
could blow my life from hers
a cell dividing without maps, sliver of ice beneath a wheel
could do the job.   Faithfulness isn't the problem.

A potato explodes in the oven.   Poetry and famine:
the poets who never starved, whose names we know
the famished nameless taking ship with their hoard of poetry
Annie Sullivan half-blind in the workhouse enthralling her child-
            mates
with lore her father had borne in his head from Limerick along
            with the dream of work
and *hatred of England smouldering like a turf-fire*. But a poetry older
            than hatred. Poetry
in the workhouse, laying of the rails, a potato splattering oven
            walls
poetry of cursing and silence, bitter and deep, shallow and
            drunken
poetry of priest-talk, of I.R.A.-talk, kitchen-talk, dream-talk,
            tongues despised
in cities where in a mere fifty years language has rotted to jargon,
            lingua franca of inclusion
from turns of speech ancient as the potato, muttered at the coals
            by women and men
rack-rented, harshened, numbed by labor ending
in root-harvest rotted in field. 1847. No relief. No succour.
America. Meat three times a day, they said.   Slaves—You would
            not be that.

VII   (THE DREAM-SITE)

Some rooftop, water-tank looming, street-racket strangely quelled
and others known and unknown there, long sweet summer eve-
                    ning on the tarred roof:
leaned back your head to the nightvault swarming with stars
the Pleiades broken loose, not seven but thousands
every known constellation flinging out fiery threads
and you could distinguish all
—cobwebs, tendrils, anatomies of stars
coherently hammocked, blueblack avenues between
—you knew your way among them, knew you were part of them
until, neck aching, you sat straight up and saw:

It was New York, the dream-site
the lost city the city of dreadful light
where once as the sacks of garbage rose
like barricades around us we
stood listening to riffs from Pharaoh Sanders' window
on the brownstone steps
went striding the avenues in our fiery hair
in our bodies young and ordinary riding the subways reading
or pressed against other bodies
feeling in them the maps of Brooklyn Queens Manhattan
The Bronx unscrolling in the long breakneck
express plunges
                    as darkly we felt our own blood
streaming   a living city overhead
coherently webbed and knotted   bristling
we and all the others
                    known and unknown
living its life

VIII

He thought there would be a limit and that it would stop him.
　　　　　He depended on that:
the cuts would be made by someone else, the direction
come from somewhere else, arrows flashing on the freeway.
That he'd end somewhere gazing
straight into It was what he imagined and nothing beyond.
That he'd end facing as limit a thing without limits and so he
　　　　　flung
and burned and hacked and bled himself toward that (if I
　　　　　understand
this story at all). What he found: FOR SALE: DO NOT
　　　　　DISTURB
OCCUPANT on some cliffs;　some ill-marked, ill-kept roads
ending in warnings about shellfish in Vietnamese, Spanish and
　　　　　English.
But the spray was any color he could have dreamed
—gold, ash, azure, smoke, moonstone—
and from time to time the ocean swirled up through the eye of a
　　　　　rock and taught him
limits.　Throwing itself backward, singing and sucking, no
　　　　　teacher, only its violent
self, the Pacific, dialectical waters rearing
their wild calm constructs, momentary, ancient.

———————　O　———————

If your voice could overwhelm those waters, what would it say?
What would it cry of the child swept under, the mother
on the beach then, in her black bathing suit, walking straight
　　　　　out
into the glazed lace as if she never noticed, what would it say of
　　　　　the father
facing inland in his shoes and socks at the edge of the tide,
what of the lost necklace glittering twisted in foam?

17

If your voice could crack in the wind hold its breath still as the
        rocks
what would it say to the daughter searching the tidelines for a
        bottled message
from the sunken slaveships?   what of the huge sun slowly de-
        faulting into the clouds
what of the picnic stored in the dunes at high tide, full of the
        moon, the basket
with sandwiches, eggs, paper napkins, can-opener, the meal
packed for a family feast, excavated now by scuttling
ants, sandcrabs, dune-rats, because no one understood
all picnics are eaten on the grave?

IX

On this earth, in this life, as I read your story, you're lonely.
Lonely in the bar, on the shore of the coastal river
with your best friend, his wife, and your wife, fishing
lonely in the prairie classroom with all the students who love
                    you. You know some ghosts
come everywhere with you yet leave them unaddressed
for years.   You spend weeks in a house
with a drunk, you sober, whom you love, feeling lonely.
You grieve in loneliness, and if I understand you fuck in
                    loneliness.

I wonder if this is a white man's madness.
I honor your truth and refuse to leave it at that.

What have I learned from stories of the hunt, of lonely men in
                    gangs?
But there were other stories:
one man riding the Mohave Desert
another man walking the Grand Canyon.
I thought those solitary men were happy, as ever they had been.

Indio's long avenues
of Medjool date-palm and lemon sweep to the Salton Sea
in Yucca Flats the high desert reaches higher, bleached and spare
                    of talk.
At Twentynine Palms I found the grave
of Maria Eleanor Whallon, eighteen years, dead at the watering-
                    hole in 1903, under the now fire-branded palms
Her mother travelled on alone to cook in the mining camps.

X

Soledad. = f. *Solitude, loneliness, homesickness; lonely retreat.*
Winter sun in the rosetrees.
An old Mexican with a white moustache prunes them back,
           spraying
the cut branches with dormant oil.   The old paper-bag-brown
           adobe walls
stretch apart from the rebuilt mission, in their own time.   It is
           lonely here
in the curve of the road winding through vast brown fields
           machine-engraved in furrows
of relentless precision.   In the small chapel
La Nuestra Señora de la Soledad dwells in her shallow arch
painted on either side with columns.   She is in black lace crisp
           as cinders
from head to foot.   Alone, solitary, homesick
in her lonely retreat.   Outside black olives fall and smash
littering and staining the beaten path.   The gravestones of the
           padres
are weights pressing down on the Indian artisans.   It is the sixth
           day of another war.

————————O————————

Across the freeway stands another structure
from the other side of the mirror   *it destroys*
the logical processes of the mind, a man's thoughts
become completely disorganized, madness streaming from every throat
frustrated sounds from the bars, metallic sounds from the walls
the steel trays, iron beds bolted to the wall, the smells, the human waste.
To determine how men will behave once they enter prison
it is of first importance to know that prison.   (From the freeway
gun-turrets planted like water-towers in another garden, out-
           buildings spaced in winter sun

and the concrete mass beyond: who now writes letters deep in-
            side that cave?)

If my instructor tells me that the world and its affairs
are run as well as they possibly can be, that I am governed
by wise and judicious men, that I am free and should be happy,
and if when I leave the instructor's presence and encounter
the exact opposite, if I actually sense or see confusion, war,
recession, depression, death and decay, is it not reasonable
that I should become perplexed?

                    From eighteen to twenty-eight
                        of his years
a young man schools himself, argues,
debates, trains, lectures to himself,
teaches himself Swahili, Spanish, learns
five new words of English every day,
chainsmokes, reads, writes letters.
In this college of force he wrestles bitterness,
self-hatred, sexual anger, cures his own nature.
Seven of these years in solitary.   Soledad.

But the significant feature of the desperate man reveals itself
when he meets other desperate men, directly or vicariously;
and he experiences his first kindness, someone to strain with him,
to strain to see him as he strains to see himself,
someone to understand, someone to accept the regard,
the love, that desperation forces into hiding.
Those feelings that find no expression in desperate times
store themselves up in great abundance, ripen, strengthen,
and strain the walls of their repository to the utmost;
where the kindred spirit touches this wall it crumbles—
no one responds to kindness, no one is more sensitive to it
than the desperate man.

XI

One night on Monterey Bay the death-freeze of the century:
a precise, detached calliper-grip holds the stars and the quarter-
        moon
in arrest: the hardiest plants crouch shrunken, a "killing frost"
on bougainvillea, Pride of Madeira, roseate black-purple succu-
        lents bowed
juices sucked awry in one orgy of freezing
slumped on their stems like old faces evicted from cheap hotels
—*into the streets of the universe, now!*

Earthquake and drought followed by freezing followed by war.
Flags are blossoming now where little else is blossoming
and I am bent on fathoming what it means to love my country.
The history of this earth and the bones within it?
Soils and cities, promises made and mocked, plowed contours of
        shame and of hope?
Loyalties, symbols, murmurs extinguished and echoing?
Grids of states stretching westward, underground waters?
Minerals, traces, rumors I am made from, morsel, minuscule
        fibre, one woman
like and unlike so many, fooled as to her destiny, the scope of
        her task?
One citizen like and unlike so many, touched and untouched in
        passing
—each of us now a driven grain, a nucleus, a city in crisis
some busy constructing enclosures, bunkers, to escape the com-
        mon fate
some trying to revive dead statues to lead us, breathing their
        breath against marble lips
some who try to teach the moment, some who preach the
        moment
some who aggrandize, some who diminish themselves in the face
        of half-grasped events

—power and powerlessness run amuck, a tape reeling backward
        in jeering, screeching syllables—
some for whom war is new, others for whom it merely continues
        the old paroxysms of time
some marching for peace who for twenty years did not march for
        justice
some for whom peace is a white man's word and a white man's
        privilege
some who have learned to handle and contemplate the shapes of
        powerlessness and power
as the nurse learns hip and thigh and weight of the body he has
        to lift and sponge, day upon day
as she blows with her every skill on the spirit's embers still burn-
        ing by their own laws in the bed of death.
A patriot is not a weapon.   A patriot is one who wrestles for the
        soul of her country
as she wrestles for her own being, for the soul of his country
(gazing through the great circle at Window Rock into the sheen
        of the Viet Nam Wall)
as he wrestles for his own being.   A patriot is a citizen trying to
        wake
from the burnt-out dream of innocence, the nightmare
of the white general and the Black general posed in their
        camouflage,
to remember her true country, remember his suffering land:
        remember
that blessing and cursing are born as twins and separated at birth
        to meet again in mourning
that the internal emigrant is the most homesick of all women and
        of all men
that every flag that flies today is a cry of pain.
                Where are we moored?
                What are the bindings?
                What behooves us?

2 3

XII

What homage will be paid to a beauty built to last
from inside out, executing the blueprints of resistance and mercy
drawn up in childhood, in that little girl, round-faced with
                clenched fists, already acquainted with mourning
in the creased snapshot you gave me?   What homage will be
                paid to beauty
that insists on speaking truth, knows the two are not always the
                same,
beauty that won't deny, is itself an eye, will not rest under
                contemplation?
Those low long clouds we were driving under a month ago in
                New Mexico, clouds an arm's reach away
were beautiful and we spoke of it but I didn't speak then
of your beauty at the wheel beside me, dark head steady, eyes
                drinking the spaces
of crimson, indigo, Indian distance, Indian presence,
your spirit's gaze informing your body, impatient to mark what's
                possible, impatient to mark
what's lost, deliberately destroyed, can never any way be
                returned,
your back arched against all icons, simulations, dead letters
your woman's hands turning the wheel or working with shears,
                torque wrench, knives, with salt pork, onions, ink
                and fire
your providing sensate hands, your hands of oak and silk, of
                blackberry juice and drums
—I speak of them now.

(FOR M.)

24

XIII   (DEDICATIONS)

I know you are reading this poem
late, before leaving your office
of the one intense yellow lamp-spot and the darkening window
in the lassitude of a building faded to quiet
long after rush-hour.   I know you are reading this poem
standing up in a bookstore far from the ocean
on a grey day of early spring, faint flakes driven
across the plains' enormous spaces around you.
I know you are reading this poem
in a room where too much has happened for you to bear
where the bedclothes lie in stagnant coils on the bed
and the open valise speaks of flight
but you cannot leave yet.   I know you are reading this poem
as the underground train loses momentum and before running
                    up the stairs
toward a new kind of love
your life has never allowed.
I know you are reading this poem by the light
of the television screen where soundless images jerk and slide
while you wait for the newscast from the *intifada*.
I know you are reading this poem in a waiting-room
of eyes met and unmeeting, of identity with strangers.
I know you are reading this poem by fluorescent light
in the boredom and fatigue of the young who are counted out,
count themselves out, at too early an age.   I know
you are reading this poem through your failing sight, the thick
lens enlarging these letters beyond all meaning yet you read on
because even the alphabet is precious.

I know you are reading this poem as you pace beside the stove
warming milk, a crying child on your shoulder, a book in your
                hand
because life is short and you too are thirsty.
I know you are reading this poem which is not in your language
guessing at some words while others keep you reading
and I want to know which words they are.
I know you are reading this poem listening for something, torn
                between bitterness and hope
turning back once again to the task you cannot refuse.
I know you are reading this poem because there is nothing else
                left to read
there where you have landed, stripped as you are.

1990–1991

———————— O ————————

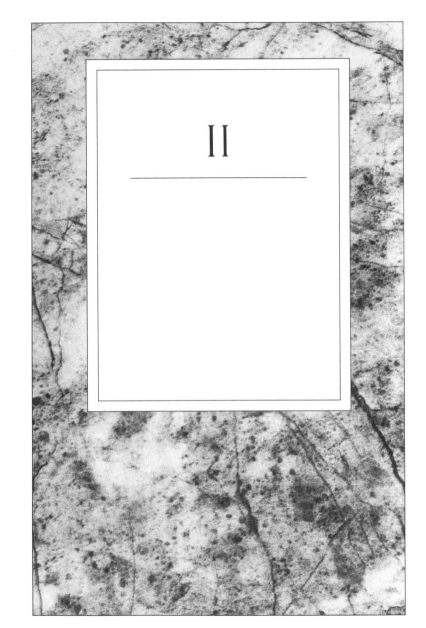

II

SHE

goes through what must be gone through:
that catalogue she is pitching out
mildew spores   velvet between the tiles
soft hairs, nests, webs
in corners, edges of basins, in the teeth
of her very comb.   All that rots or rusts
in a night, a century.
Balances memory, training, sits in her chair
hairbrush in hand, breathing the scent of her own hair
and thinks: *I have been the weir*
where disintegration stopped.
Lifts her brush once like a thrown thing
lays it down at her side like a stockpiled weapon
crushes out the light.   Elsewhere
dust chokes the filters, dead leaves rasp in the grate.
Clogged, the fine nets bulge
and she is not there.

1988

THAT MOUTH

This is the girl's mouth, the taste
daughters, not sons, obtain:
These are the lips, powerful rudders
pushing through groves of kelp,
the girl's terrible, unsweetened taste
of the whole ocean, its fathoms: this is that taste.

This is not the father's kiss, the mother's:
a father can try to choke you,
a mother drown you to save you:
all the transactions have long been enacted.
This is neither a sister's tale nor a brother's:
strange trade-offs have long been made.

This is the swallow, the splash
of krill and plankton, that mouth
described as a girl's—
enough to give you a taste:
Are you a daughter, are you a son?
Strange trade-offs have long been made.

1988

MARGHANITA

at the oak table under the ceiling fan
Marghanita at the table counting up
a dead woman's debts.
Kicks off a sandal, sips
soda from a can, wedges the last bills
under the candelabrum.   She is here
because no one else was there when worn-to-skeleton
her enemy died.   Her love.   Her twin.
Marghanita dreamed the intravenous, the intensive
the stainless steel
before she ever saw them.   She's not practical,
you know, they used to say.
She's the artist, she got away.

In her own place Marghanita glues bronze
feathers into wings, smashes green and clear
bottles into bloodletting particles
crushed into templates of sand
scores mirrors till they fall apart and sticks them up
in driftwood boughs, drinks golden
liquid with a worm's name, forgets
her main enemy, her twin;
scores her wrist on a birthday
dreams the hospital dream.

When they were girl and boy together, boy and girl
she pinned his arm against his back
for a box containing false
lashes and fingernails, a set of veils, a string of pearls,

she let go and listened to his tales
she breathed their breath, he hers,
they each had names only the other knew.

Marghanita in the apartment everyone has left:
not a nephew, not a niece,
nobody from the parish
—gone into hiding, emigrated, lost?
where are the others?
Marghanita comes back because she does,
adding up what's left:
a rainsoaked checkbook, snapshots
razed from an album,
colors ground into powder, brushes, wands
for eyelids, lashes, brows,
beads of bath-oil, tubes of glycerin
—a dead woman's luxuries.

Marghanita will
take care of it all.   Pay if nothing else
the last month's rent.   The wings of the fan
stir corners of loose paper,
light ebbs from the window-lace,
she needs to go out and eat.   And so
hating and loving come down
to a few columns of figures,
an aching stomach, a care taken: something done.

1989

OLIVIA

"Among fundamentalist Christians, she was one of them;
in our anti-apartheid groups, she was the
most militant. . . . She was a chameleon." —White
South African student activist interviewed on National Public Radio, 10/11/88

Yes, I saw you, see you, come
into the meetings, out of the rain
with your wan cheek and your thin waist—
did anyone see you eat?

Did anyone see you eat, did you wear
a woman's body, were you air
to their purpose, liquid at their call
when you stood, spine against the wall?

And I know your stance, back to the wall,
overlooking the others, your bent head
your sense of timing, your outraged tongue
the notes you take when you get home.

I see the white joints of your wrist
moving across the yellow pad
the exhausted theatre of your sleep:
I know the power you thought you had—

to know them all, better than they
knew you, than they knew you knew,
to know better than those who paid
you—paid by them, to move

at some pure point of mastery
as if, in your slight outline, moon
you could dwell above them, light and shade,
travel forever to and fro

above both sides, all sides, none,
gliding the edges, knapsack crammed
—was that it? to lift above
loyalty, love and all that trash

higher than power and its fields of force?
—never so much as a woman friend?
You were a woman walked on a leash.
And they dropped you in the end.

1988

EASTERN WAR TIME

1

Memory lifts her smoky mirror: 1943,
single isinglass window   kerosene
stove in the streetcar barn   halfset moon
8:15 a.m. Eastern War Time dark
Number 29 clanging in and turning
looseleaf notebook   *Latin for Americans*
Breasted's *History of the Ancient World*
on the girl's lap
money for lunch and war-stamps in her pocket
darkblue wool wet acrid on her hands
three pools of light   weak ceiling bulbs
a schoolgirl's hope-spilt terrified
sensations wired to smells
of kerosene wool and snow
and the sound of the dead language
praised as key   torchlight of the great dead
Grey spreading   behind still-flying snow
the lean and sway of the streetcar she must ride
to become one   of a hundred girls
rising white-cuffed and collared in a study hall
to sing *For those in peril on the sea*
under plaster casts of the classic frescoes
chariots horses draperies certitudes.

2

Girl between home and school   what is that girl
swinging her plaid linen bookbag   what's an American girl
in wartime   her permed friz of hair
her glasses for school and movies
between school and home   ignorantly Jewish
trying to grasp the world
through books: *Jude the Obscure   The Ballad
of Reading Gaol*   Eleanor Roosevelt's *My Story*

NV15   CABLE-LIVERPOOL   122   1/63NFD
HEADQUARTERS PLAN DISCUSSED AND UNDER
                CONSIDERATION
ALL JEWS IN COUNTRIES OCCUPIED OR CONTROLLED
                GERMANY
NUMBER 3½ - TO 4 MILLION SHOULD AFTER
                DEPORTATION
AND CONCENTRATION IN EAST
AT ONE BLOW EXTERMINATED TO RESOLVE
ONCE AND FOR ALL JEWISH QUESTION IN EUROPE

3
How telegrams used to come: ring
of the doorbell   serious messenger
bicycling with his sheaf   enveloped pasted strips
yellow on yellow   the stripped messages
DELAYED STOP MEET 2:27 THURSDAY
DAUGHTER BORN LAST NIGHT STOP BOTH DOING
              WELL
THE WAR DEPARTMENT REGRETS TO INFORM YOU
also: PARENTS DEPORTED UNKNOWN DESTINATION
              EAST
SITUATION DIFFICULT   ether of messages
in capital letters   silence

4
What the grown-ups can't speak of   would you push
onto children?   and the deadweight of Leo Frank
thirty years lynched   hangs heavy
:   "this is what our parents were trying to spare us"   :
here in America   but in terrible Europe
anything was possible   surely?
:   "But this is the twentieth century"   :
what the grown-ups can't teach   children must learn
how do you teach a child what you won't believe?
how do you say   *unfold, my flower, shine, my star*
and *we are hated, being what we are?*

5
A young girl knows she is young and meant to live
taken on the closed journey
her pockets drained of meaning
her ankles greased in vomit and diarrhea
driven naked across the yard
a young girl remembers her youth:
anything   textbooks   forbidden novels
school songs   petnames
the single time she bled and never since
having her hair done   its pale friz
clipped and shaped   still friz   pale Jewish hair
over her green Jewish eyes
thinking she was pretty and that others would see it
and not to bleed again and not to die
in the gas   but on the operating table
of the famous doctor
who plays string quartets with his staff in the laboratory

6

A girl wanders with a boy into the woods
a romantic walk   a couple in a poem
hand-in-hand   but you're not watching each other
for signs of desire   you're watching the woods
for signs of the secret bases   lines
converging toward the resistance   where the guns
are cached   the precious tools
the strategies argued   you're fourteen, fifteen
classmates from Vilna   walking away from Vilna
your best marks were in history and geometry   his
in chemistry   you don't intend to die
too much you think is waiting in you   for you
you never knew the forest outside Vilna
could hide so many   would have to
you'd dreamed of living in the forest
as in a folksong   lying on loose pine-needles
light ribboning from sky cross-hatched with needles
you and one dearest friend   now you will meet the others

7
A woman of sixty   driving
the great grades   sea-level to high desert
a century slipping from her shoulders
a blink in geological time
though heavy to those who had to wear it
Knowledge has entered her connective tissue and
into sand dissolved her cartilage
If her skeleton is found this will be clear
or was it knowledge   maybe a dangerous questioning
At night she lies   eyes open   seeing
the young who do not wander in the moonlight
as in a poem   faces seen
for thirty years   under the fire-hoses
walking through mobs to school
dragged singing from the buses
following the coffins
and here   brows knotted under knotted scarfs
dark eyes   searching armed streets
for the end of degradation

8

A woman wired in memories
stands by a house   collapsed in dust
her son beaten in prison   grandson
shot in the stomach   daughter
organizing the camps   an aunt's unpublished poems
grandparents' photographs   a bridal veil
phased into smoke   up the obliterate air
With whom shall she let down and tell her story
Who shall hear her to the end
standing if need be for hours   in wind
that swirls the levelled dust
in sun that beats through their scarfed hair
at the lost gate by the shattered prickly pear
Who must hear her to the end
but the woman   forbidden to forget
the blunt groats freezing in the wooden ladle
old winds   dusting the ovens with light snow?

9
Streets closed, emptied by force   Guns at corners
with open mouths and eyes   Memory speaks:
You cannot live on me alone
you cannot live without me
I'm nothing if I'm just a roll of film
stills from a vanished world
fixed lightstreaked mute
left for another generation's
restoration and framing   I can't be restored or framed
I can't be still   I'm here
in your mirror   pressed leg to leg beside you
intrusive inappropriate bitter flashing
with what makes me unkillable though killed

10

Memory says: Want to do right? Don't count on me.
I'm a canal in Europe where bodies are floating
I'm a mass grave   I'm the life that returns
I'm a table set with room for the Stranger
I'm a field with corners left for the landless
I'm accused of child-death   of drinking blood
I'm a man-child praising God he's a man
I'm a woman bargaining for a chicken
I'm a woman who sells for a boat ticket
I'm a family dispersed between night and fog
I'm an immigrant tailor who says *A coat
is not a piece of cloth only*   I sway
in the learnings of the master-mystics
I have dreamed of Zion   I've dreamed of world revolution
I have dreamed my children could live at last like others
I have walked the children of others through ranks of hatred
I'm a corpse dredged from a canal in Berlin
a river in Mississippi   I'm a woman standing
with other women dressed in black
on the streets of Haifa, Tel Aviv, Jerusalem
there is spit on my sleeve there are phonecalls in the night
I am a woman standing in line for gasmasks
I stand on a road in Ramallah   with naked face   listening
I am standing here in your poem   unsatisfied
lifting my smoky mirror

1989–1990

44

TATTERED KADDISH

Taurean reaper of the wild apple field
messenger from earthmire gleaning
transcripts of fog
in the nineteenth year and the eleventh month
speak your tattered Kaddish for all suicides:

Praise to life though it crumbled in like a tunnel
on ones we knew and loved

> Praise to life though its windows blew shut
> on the breathing-room of ones we knew and loved

Praise to life though ones we knew and loved
loved it badly, too well, and not enough

> Praise to life though it tightened like a knot
> on the hearts of ones we thought we knew loved us

Praise to life giving room and reason
to ones we knew and loved who felt unpraisable

> Praise to them, how they loved it, when they could.

1989

THROUGH CORRALITOS UNDER ROLLS OF CLOUD

I
Through Corralitos under rolls of cloud
between winter-stiff, ranged apple-trees
each netted in transparent air,
thin sinking light, heartsick within and filmed
in heartsickness around you, gelatin cocoon
invisible yet impervious—to the hawk
steering against the cloudbank, to the clear
oranges burning at the rancher's gate
rosetree, agave, stiff beauties holding fast
with or without your passion,
the pruners freeing up the boughs
in the unsearched faith these strange stiff shapes will bear.

II

Showering after 'flu;   stripping the bed;
running the shrouds of sickness through the wash;
airing the rooms;   emptying the trash;
it's as if part of you had died in the house
sometime in that last low-lit afternoon
when your dreams ebbed salt-thick into the sheets
and now this other's left to wash the corpse,
burn eucalyptus, turn the mirrors over—
this other who herself barely came back,
whose breath was fog to your mist, whose stubborn shadow
covered you as you lay freezing, she survived
uncertain who she is or will be without you.

III

If you know who died in that bed, do you know
who has survived?   If you say, *she was weaker,*
held life less dear, expected others
to fight for her   if pride lets you name her
victim   and the one who got up and threw
the windows open, stripped the bed, *survivor*
—what have you said, what do you know
of the survivor when you know her
only in opposition to the lost?
What does it mean to say *I have survived*
until you take the mirrors and turn them outward
and read your own face in their outraged light?

IV

That light of outrage is the light of history
springing upon us when we're least prepared,
thinking maybe a little glade of time
leaf-thick and with clear water
is ours, is promised us, for all we've hacked
and tracked our way through: to this:
What will it be?   Your wish or mine?   your
prayers or my wish then: that those we love
be well, whatever that means, to be well.
Outrage: who dare claim protection for their own
amid such unprotection?   What kind of prayer
is that?   To what kind of god?   What kind of wish?

V

She who died on that bed sees it her way:
She who went under peers through the translucent shell
cupping her death and sees her other well,
through a long lens, in silvered outline, well
she sees her other and she cannot tell
why when the boom of surf struck at them both
she felt the undertow and heard the bell,
thought death would be their twinning, till the swell
smashed her against the reef, her other still
fighting the pull, struggling somewhere away
further and further, calling her all the while:
she who went under summons her other still.

1989–1990

FOR A FRIEND IN TRAVAIL

Waking from violence: the surgeon's probe left in the foot
paralyzing the body from the waist down.
Dark before dawn: wrapped in a shawl, to walk the house
the Drinking-Gourd slung in the northwest,
half-slice of moon to the south
through dark panes.   A time to speak to you.

What are you going through? she said, is the great question.
Philosopher of oppression, theorist
of the victories of force.

We write from the marrow of our bones.   What she did not
ask, or tell: how victims save their own lives.

That crawl along the ledge, then the ravelling span of fibre
                        strung
from one side to the other, I've dreamed that too.
Waking, not sure we made it.   Relief, appallment, of waking.
Consciousness.   O, no.   To sleep again.
O to sleep without dreaming.

How day breaks, when it breaks, how clear and light the moon
melting into moon-colored air
moist and sweet, here on the western edge.
Love for the world, and we are part of it.
How the poppies break from their sealed envelopes
she did not tell.

What are you going through, there on the other edge?

1990

1948: JEWS

A mother's letter, torn open
in a college mailroom:
. . . *Some of them will be*
the most brilliant, fascinating
you'll ever meet
but don't get taken up by any clique
trying to claim you

—Marry out, like your father
she didn't write   She wrote for   wrote
against   him

It was a burden for anyone
to be fascinating, brilliant
after the six million
Never mind just coming home
and trying to get some sleep
like an ordinary person

1990

TWO ARTS

1

I've redone you by daylight.
Squatted before your gauntness
chipping away.   Slivers of rock
piling up like petals.
All night I'd worked to illuminate the skull.
By dawn you were pure electric.   You pulsed like a star.
You awoke in the last darkness
before the light poured in.
I've redone you by daylight.

Now I can submit you to the arts administrator
and the council of patrons
who could never take your measure.
This time they will love you,
standing on the glass table, fluent and robed at last,
and all your origins countered.
I wrap you in pure white sheets to mail you,
I brush you off my apron,
the charged filings crunch like cinders on the floor.

2

Raise it up there and it will
loom, the gaunt original thing
gristle and membrane of your life
mortared with shells of trilobites
it will hold between the cracks
of lightning, in the deadpan face of before and after
it will stick on up there as you left it
pieced together by starlight
it will hang by the flying buttresses you gave it
—hulk of mist, rafter of air, suspension bridge of mica
helm of sweat and dew—
but you have to raise it up there, you
have a brutal thing to do.

1990

DARKLIGHT

I
Early day.   Grey the air.
Grey the boards of the house, the bench,
red the dilated potflower's petals
blue the sky that will rend through
this fog.
        Dark summer's outer reaches:
thrown husk of a moon
sharpening
in the last dark blue.
I think of your eye
               (dark the light
that washes into a deeper dark).

An eye, coming in closer.
              Under the lens
lashes and veins grow huge
and huge the tear that washes out the eye,
the tear that clears the eye.

II
When heat leaves the walls at last
and the breeze comes
or seems to come, off water
or off the half-finished moon
her silver roughened by a darkblue rag
this is the ancient hour
between light and dark, work and rest
earthly tracks and star-trails
the last willed act of the day
and the night's first dream

If you could have this hour
for the last hour of your life.

1988–1990

FINAL NOTATIONS

it will not be simple, it will not be long
it will take little time, it will take all your thought
it will take all your heart, it will take all your breath
it will be short, it will not be simple

it will touch through your ribs, it will take all your heart
it will not be long, it will occupy your thought
as a city is occupied, as a bed is occupied
it will take all your flesh, it will not be simple

You are coming into us who cannot withstand you
you are coming into us who never wanted to withstand you
you are taking parts of us into places never planned
you are going far away with pieces of our lives

it will be short, it will take all your breath
it will not be simple, it will become your will

1991

NOTES

"An Atlas of the Difficult World, V": "over the chained bay waters."
From Hart Crane, "To Brooklyn Bridge," in *The Poems of Hart Crane*, ed.
Marc Simon (New York and London: Liveright, 1989; poem originally
published in 1930). "There are roads to take when you think of your
country." From Muriel Rukeyser, *U.S. 1* (New York: Covici Friede, 1938);
see also Muriel Rukeyser, *The Collected Poems* (New York: McGraw-Hill,
1978). "I don't want to know how he tracked them." On May 13, 1988,
Stephen Roy Carr shot and killed Rebecca Wight, one of two lesbians
camping on the Appalachian Trail in Pennsylvania. Her lover, Claudia
Brenner, suffered five bullet wounds. She dragged herself two miles along
the trail to a road, where she flagged a car to take her to the police. In
October of that year, Carr was found guilty of first-degree murder and
sentenced to life in prison without parole. During the legal proceedings,
it became clear that Carr had attacked the women because they were
lesbians. See *Gay Community News* (August 7 and November 11, 1988).

"An Atlas of the Difficult World, VI": "hatred of England smouldering
like a turf-fire." See Nella Braddy, *Anne Sullivan Macy: The Story behind
Helen Keller* (Garden City, N.Y.: Doubleday, Doran & Company, 1933),
p. 13. "Meat three times a day." See Frank Murray, "The Irish and Afro-
Americans in U.S. History," *Freedomways: A Quarterly Review of the Freedom
Movement* 22, no. 1 (1982): 22.

"An Atlas of the Difficult World, X": The passages in italics are quoted
from *Soledad Brother: The Prison Letters of George Jackson* (New York: Bantam,
1970), pp. 24, 26, 93, 245.

"Eastern War Time, 2": Text of a telegram sent through the American
legation in Bern, Switzerland, August 11, 1942, to the U.S. State De-
partment in Washington, and transmitted after several weeks' delay to
Rabbi Stephen Wise in New York. See David S. Wyman, *The Abandonment
of the Jews* (New York: Pantheon, 1984), pp. 42–45.

"Eastern War Time, 4": Charged with the murder of a fourteen-year-
old girl employed in his uncle's pencil factory in Atlanta, Leo Max Frank
(1884–1915), a mechanical engineer, was tried and found guilty, and the
decision appealed, in a climate of intense anti-Semitism. When his sentence

was commuted from death to life by the governor of Georgia, he was dragged by a mob from prison and lynched.

"Eastern War Time, 10": "A coat is not a piece of cloth only." See Barbara Myerhoff, *Number Our Days* (New York: Simon & Schuster, 1978), p. 44. Myerhoff quotes Shmuel Goldman, immigrant Socialist garment-worker: "It is not the way of a Jew to make his work like there was no human being to suffer when it's done badly. A coat is not a piece of cloth only. The tailor is connected to the one who wears it and he should not forget it."

"Tattered Kaddish": "The Reapers of the Field are the Comrades, masters of this wisdom, because *Malkhut* is called the Apple Field, and She grows sprouts of secrets and new meanings of Torah. Those who constantly create new interpretations of Torah are the ones who reap Her" (Moses Cordovero, Or ha-Hammah on Zohar III, 106a). See Barry W. Holtz, ed., *Back to the Sources: Reading the Classic Jewish Texts* (New York: Summit, 1984), p. 305.

"For a Friend in Travail": "The love of our neighbor in all its fullness simply means being able to say to him: 'What are you going through?' " Simone Weil, *Waiting for God* (New York: Putnam, 1951), p. 115.